Wouldn't It Be Nice If . . . ?

Skillfully written by Alaskan author, Billy Ray Macon Sr., WOULDN'T IT BE NICE IF. . . is primarily about "thought". Deep thought, with a dash of levity. Just think about how nice it would be to look at, take note of, participate in things you have noticed, but from a unique viewpoint. This is a dream book for the mind. Dare to attempt things that may never come, but then. . . you never know. Dare to challenge the art of deep thought, live the dare, love the ride, just think about it. Wouldn't It Be Nice If? You will certainly enjoy this read!

Wouldn't It Be Nice If . . . ?

Billy Ray Macon Sr.

To order additional copies of this book, contact:
Xlibris Corporation
1-888-795-4274
www.Xlibris.com
Orders@Xlibris.com
66030

DEDICATED TO LOURDES MARIE MACON.

I dedicate Wouldn't It Be Nice If . . . . To my beautiful bride of 51 Years, who believed in me 51 years ago when we dreamt and talked about how nice it would be to move to Alaska to begin a life together as one. To my best friend, thank you for sharing the magic and memories of life!—

WOULDN'T IT BE NICE IF . . . ?

LIFE

Wouldn't it be nice if,
> People were flat out "nice"?

Wouldn't it be nice if,
> T.V. stood for "truth viewers"?

Wouldn't it be nice if,
> The more you talked, the sharper you got?

Wouldn't it be nice if,
> All people could experience the majesty of the great State of Alaska?

Wouldn't it be nice if,
>   One could write his or her way out of a negative situation?

Wouldn't it be nice if,
>   Your memory never failed you?

Wouldn't it be nice if,
>   When we complain we have no shoes, we are reminded of those who have no feet?

Wouldn't it be nice if,
>   Everyone I said "good morning" to would convey that good morning to at least thirty others?

Wouldn't it be nice if,
>   Tomorrows never ran out?

Wouldn't it be nice if,
>   When you make the statement "God Bless You" you meant it even if you weren't in the best of moods?

Wouldn't it be nice if,
>   Every friend you've ever made was more that friend today that he or she has ever been?

Wouldn't it be nice if,
>   Every time someone said please, someone said "thank you"?

Wouldn't it be nice if,
>The term "you scratch my back and I'll scratch yours" simply meant we had an itch?

Wouldn't it be nice if,
>Your fellow motorist would have the same respect you were taught to show them?

Wouldn't it be nice if,
>When you said "no" people accepted that?

Wouldn't it be nice if,
>The last aids patient diagnosed, cured yesterday?

Wouldn't it be nice if,
>A switch could turn off a heart ache?

Wouldn't it be nice if,
>You could erase obesity?

Wouldn't it be nice if,
>You could come to me and I could reassure you that man will not eventually wipe out all life forms on earth?

Wouldn't it be nice if,
>We could have a disagreement, shake hands and still be friends tomorrow?

Wouldn't it be nice if,
>Celebrity marriages had a chance for longevity?

Wouldn't it be nice if,

> That restful night sleep you had last night was an indicator of many more to come in the future?

Wouldn't it be nice if,

> Cancer could be cured as easy as your sore throat?

Wouldn't it be nice if,

> All it took to be comfortable is hard work?

Wouldn't it be nice if,

> You could be an American and not have the fear of acts of harassment?

Wouldn't it be nice if,

> The elderly would be referred to as the wise ones?

Wouldn't it be nice if,

> I who have nothing, could have something?

Wouldn't it be nice if,

> Your need to need was fulfilled by someone you need?

Wouldn't it be nice if,

> The respect between you and your neighbor was there, even without the fence?

Wouldn't it be nice if,

> Instead of cloning, man was clowning?

Wouldn't it be nice if,
> The fourth of July was the fourth of every month?

Wouldn't it be nice if,
> Common sense came in a bottle?

Wouldn't it be nice if,
> When you are shaking hands you were actually shaking my hand?

Wouldn't it be nice if,
> We were rewarded for not breaking the law, rather than be punished for breaking the law—which is more economical?

Wouldn't it be nice if,
> After supplying 10 men with 100 dollars each, the 100 dollars wouldn't end up in just one or two pockets?

Wouldn't it be nice if,
> Vacations were not so expensive?

Wouldn't it be nice if,
> An apple a day really did keep the doctor away?

Wouldn't it be nice if,
> People believed their grass was a good shade of green and not run to the other side?

Wouldn't it be nice if,
> One could reach their potential more often than not?

Wouldn't it be nice if,
>A fallen star could crush all negativity?

Wouldn't it be nice if,
>Gas could afford me?

Wouldn't it be nice if,
>There was a nation of Oprah Winfrey's?

Wouldn't it be nice if,
>The fact that we have so many pain killers; we could have the intelligence to invent an 800 milligram pill to kill cancer?

Wouldn't it be nice if,
>Oprah's love was contagious and most hate mongers would catch it?

Wouldn't it be nice if,
>You could really think and grow rich?

Wouldn't it be nice if,
>Global warming had a knob marked cool?

Wouldn't it be nice if,
>Some trees of summer could have some colors of fall?

Wouldn't it be nice if,
>There were no issues contributing to the gender gap?

Wouldn't it be nice if,
>The simple things in life were still simple?

Wouldn't it be nice if,
>The last money you loaned was in reality a gift?

Wouldn't it be nice if,
>The results of a restful nights sleep could be passed on to a less fortunate individual?

Wouldn't it be nice if,
>From a mental point of view you turn a corner and met yourself coming?

Wouldn't it be nice if,
>There was such a thing as a 55 gallon drum of Oprah love?

Wouldn't it be nice if,
>Talent shows up in your everyday work performance?

Wouldn't it be nice if,
>You could hear a bird sing and understand it?

Wouldn't it be nice if,
>Pain could be turned off like a light switch?

Wouldn't it be nice if,
>You have what I have, and I have what you have and there is no envy or jealousy?

Wouldn't it be nice if,
>When you pass a stranger on the street, you don't have a feeling of fear, but rather

a feeling of just how wonderful it is to be a part of the human race?

Wouldn't it be nice if,
> Trees could talk and give us heads up when fall is coming?

Wouldn't it be nice if,
> Physical fitness fit your necessary needs?

Wouldn't it be nice if,
> The best golf advice you ever received was really the best?

Wouldn't it be nice if,
> People would find other way to vent their frustrations other than &*^##@?

Wouldn't it be nice if,
> Nothing ever happened to the brave?

Wouldn't it be nice if,
> Every young girl would aspire to become an Oprah Winfrey—the woman's woman?

Wouldn't it be nice if,
> Gas prices fell while the wages rose?

Wouldn't it be nice if,
> The end of time wasn't the end of time itself?

Wouldn't it be nice if,
> The challenges of life were a little less challenging?

Wouldn't it be nice if,
>   We could all deal with life with three simple principles: live, laugh and love?

Wouldn't it be nice if,
>   The grass was never thought to be greener on the other side?

Wouldn't it be nice if,
>   Time could sometimes be slowed down?

Wouldn't it be nice if,
>   We all understood progress is not perfection—its progress?

Wouldn't it be nice if,
>   More he's and she's became "we"?

Wouldn't it be nice if,
>   You could consistently go to sleep when you go to bed?

Wouldn't it be nice if,
>   We always gave it all we've got?

Wouldn't it be nice if,
>   Poetry could be a walkway above the strifes of life?

Wouldn't it be nice if,
>   Poetry could be an extension of one's emotions?

Wouldn't it be nice if,
> People could say what they were unable to say?

Wouldn't it be nice if,
> The law of increasing returns would hurry up and return?

Wouldn't it be nice if,
> Great, was something everyone could be without having to try so hard?

Wouldn't it be nice if,
> More T.V. news reporters had the class embedded in such news soldiers as Keith Oberman, Rachel Maddow, Chris Matthews and Ed Shultz? (But not necessarily in that order.)

Wouldn't it be nice if,
> The law would do something about the vicious dogs next door?

Wouldn't it be nice if,
> Common sense was standard equipment?

Wouldn't it be nice if,
> Instead of reacting to violence with violence, you follow the letter of the law?

Wouldn't it be nice if,
> More people were nice and easily approachable?

Wouldn't it be nice if,
> Mankind did a better job of governing himself?

Wouldn't it be nice if,
> A computer could make you be the best you could be?

Wouldn't it be nice if,
> You feared your conscious more than your fellow man?

Wouldn't it be nice if,
> Those who have nothing could get a little something other than condemnation?

Wouldn't it be nice if,
> Airport security had a uniform code?

Wouldn't it be nice if,
> Laws were unnecessary?

Wouldn't it be nice if,
> When one visited another country, he or she doesn't feel like a foreigner?

Wouldn't it be nice if,
> Half of the negative things that come out of your mouth would have only been thought about, instead?

Wouldn't it be nice if,
> You would have remembered yesterday to remind yourself of the important duties that need today's attention?

Wouldn't it be nice if,
> You were you, for real?

Wouldn't it be nice if,
> You could hold life together with a paper clip?

Wouldn't it be nice if,
> You didn't have to worry about anything?

Wouldn't it be nice if,
> You could flick a switch and change your life for the better?

Wouldn't it be nice if,
> When you attempted to cross the street you made it?

Wouldn't it be nice if,
> You were about to say something negative and didn't?

Wouldn't it be nice if,
> A law enforcement officer with just a glance, could get his or her point across?

Wouldn't it be nice if,
> Bad luck could be converted to cash?

Wouldn't it be nice if,
> The music that soothes the savage beast would soothe the domestically violent?

Wouldn't it be nice if,
> We could learn from others mistakes, instead of repeating them yourself?

Wouldn't it be nice if,
> Help is what we did and not just in 911 situations?

Wouldn't it be nice if,
> You and I could just be you and I?

Wouldn't it be nice if,
> The expression "he or she did a turnaround" was more than physical?

Wouldn't it be nice if,
> "Yes I will" could be something to count on?

Wouldn't it be nice if,
> A handshake was still the "in thing"?

Wouldn't it be nice if,
> Yesterday could remain a part of the past?

Wouldn't it be nice if,
> Some of time was not mistaken for all of the time?

Wouldn't it be nice if,
> There was as much money left at the end of the month, as there was month left at the end?

Wouldn't it be nice if,
> News was news?

Wouldn't it be nice if,
> PC meant patience and courtesy?

Wouldn't it be nice if,
> Every time (not just some of the time) you gave someone a "good morning", you received one?

Wouldn't it be nice if,
> Common sense came in a bottle?

Wouldn't it be nice if,
> The crack head you knew yesterday, would stop being a crack head tomorrow?

Wouldn't it be nice if,
> You could put 100% of trust and faith in your fellow man? (But . . . man is only human.)

Wouldn't it be nice if,
> There were as many days between Friday and Monday, as there are between Monday and Friday?

Wouldn't it be nice if,
> A penny candy was a penny again?

Wouldn't it be nice if,
> I could give the time of day, and receive the r respect of the world?

Wouldn't it be nice if,
> The unemployed could experience the joy of employment at the same time?

Wouldn't it be nice if,
> Every time you sat down, rest would be guaranteed?

Wouldn't it be nice if,
> Your concerns about life were just a bit more than concerns?

Wouldn't it be nice if,
> The thought of helping my fellow man could and would become more than just a thought (a reality)?

Wouldn't it be nice if,
> The good didn't die so young?

Wouldn't it be nice if,
> Wars could be fought only on the computer?

Wouldn't it be nice if,
> Dancing would relieve the tensions of the world?

Wouldn't it be nice if,
> We would stop taking advantage of others just because we can?

Wouldn't it be nice if,
> Cancer was just a word with no meaning?

Wouldn't it be nice if,

There was as much attention paid before death as there is after?

Wouldn't it be nice if,

Freedom was a little less expensive?

Wouldn't it be nice if,

The rich were a little less rich and the poor were a little less hungry?

Wouldn't it be nice if,

You would trade a little wealth for a lot of integrity?

Wouldn't it be nice if,

You could get richer without your fellowman getting poorer?

Wouldn't it be nice if,

Everyone could live like kings and queens?

Wouldn't it be nice if,

Feed the children was something that didn't have to be prompted?

Wouldn't it be nice if,

Guns brought more happiness and less sorrow?

Wouldn't it be nice if,

Prisons created more useful citizens than harden criminals?

Wouldn't it be nice if,
> The drug runners would run the hell out of town?

Wouldn't it be nice if,
> A boot to the back of the drug dealer's pants would awake them to the ills of their deeds?

Wouldn't it be nice if,
> When a drug dealer looked at the city jail, he would sing the song *I'll Be There*?

Wouldn't it be nice if,
> A murderer wasn't?

Wouldn't it be nice if,
> An aspirin would end the pain in your mind?

Wouldn't it be nice if,
> The next time someone dies, it won't' be murder?

Wouldn't it be nice if,
> When it is time for someone to die, it would be from natural causes?

Wouldn't it be nice if,
> Law and order were one in the same?

Wouldn't it be nice if,
> Insurance companies kept their word?

Wouldn't it be nice if,
> An automobile wasn't such a dangerous weapon?

Wouldn't it be nice if,
> All police officers were like the good ones?

Wouldn't it be nice if,
> There was as much justice in some court rooms as there are people?

Wouldn't it be nice if,
> The only unemployed were those wanting it?

Wouldn't it be nice if,
> Those wanting employment could have it?

Wouldn't it be nice if,
> A bank robber had the same level of skills only on the other side of the law?

Wouldn't it be nice if,
> The word *please* did much more?

Wouldn't it be nice if,
> Helping yourself was a prelude to helping others?

Wouldn't it be nice if,
> Working in an open 24 hours a day store wasn't so dangerous?

Wouldn't it be nice if,
> The police would enforce the law without fear?

Wouldn't it be nice if,
> A flat tire was a warning of danger ahead—stop?

Wouldn't it be nice if,
> Directional safety signs were followed?

Wouldn't it be nice if,
> Doctor's advice was at least considered?

Wouldn't it be nice if,
> Everyone that wanted it could have an ID that said I am an American?

Wouldn't it be nice if,
> There had never been a Hitler?

Wouldn't it be nice if,
> There were never ever another war?

Wouldn't it be nice if,
> Every time someone tried to wage war, they would get deathly sick to their stomach?

Wouldn't it be nice if,
> Everyone's concerns were for more than themselves?

Wouldn't it be nice if,
> People thought life to be so precious they wouldn't take one?

Wouldn't it be nice if,

> The poor house didn't have so many residents?

Wouldn't it be nice if,

> Birthdays came every ten years with a one year aging process?

Wouldn't it be nice if,

> Being serious didn't have to mean being sad?

Wouldn't it be nice if,

> You could take one step forward without taking four steps back?

Wouldn't it be nice if,

> Watching television would promote integrity?

Wouldn't it be nice if,

> You were always you, regardless?

Wouldn't it be nice if,

> Racism, the Berlin Wall and crime, were all things of the past?

Wouldn't it be nice if,

> Those whom control the past will not control the future?

Wouldn't it be nice if,

> Give me a leg up automatically meant success?

Wouldn't it be nice if,
> Experiencing cold and hunger were just that, an experiment?

Wouldn't it be nice if,
> The last money you loaned, was in fact a gift?

Wouldn't it be nice if,
> The results of a restful nights sleep could be passed on to the less fortunate?

Wouldn't it be nice if,
> All you personally needed from a five dollar bill was a dollar fifty, and you gave the three fifty to someone who needed in more than you?

Wouldn't it be nice if,
> When you said goodbye it would be the beginning of a return trip?

Wouldn't it be nice if,
> When you got that second chance to be a human being, you became one?

Wouldn't it be nice if,
> The people you trusted were worthy of it?

Wouldn't it be nice if,
> The next breath of air you take was fresh?

Wouldn't it be nice if,
> Common sense came in a bottle?

Wouldn't it be nice if,
> All of the name calling would be that of your given name?

Wouldn't it be nice if,
> Whenever a question is asked, an answer would be given?

WOULDN'T IT BE NICE IF . . . ?

FAMILY

Wouldn't it be nice if,

Every time your spouse said "I Love You Dear" the children got that much closer to celebrating their Mom and Pops 50th Anniversary?

Wouldn't it be nice if,

Everyone had a Mom, as wonderful as mine?

Wouldn't it be nice if,
> New parents would watch TV and pay close attention to the parenting skills of Leave it to Beaver's Mr. Ward Cleaver?

Wouldn't it be nice if,
> Domestic violence could be stamped out with the persistence of being labeled a felon?

Wouldn't it be nice if,
> Everyone had a Grandmother as wonderful as my grandchildren's?

Wouldn't it be nice if,
> You could somehow repay your parents?

Wouldn't it be nice if,
> People would stop believing the ice cream and candy are acceptable babysitters?

Wouldn't it be nice if,
> Everyone got the chance to meet their grandparents?

Wouldn't it be nice if,
> When you did something for someone they showed their appreciation by truly appreciating it?

Wouldn't it be nice if,
> Whenever the statement was made "I Love you Son" the response is "almost as much as "I Love You Dad"?

Wouldn't it be nice if,
> You had more than one lifetime with your parents?

Wouldn't it be nice if,
> The pride you have for your parent's, encourages and instills the same pride in your children?

Wouldn't it be nice if,
> A family reunion reunited all?

Wouldn't it be nice if,
> There were national honors for great parenting?

Wouldn't it be nice if,
> Everyone experienced a mother's love?

Wouldn't it be nice if,
> You were nice even when no one expected you to be?

Wouldn't it be nice if,
> Everyone experienced a father's love?

Wouldn't it be nice if,
> Families could focus on family?

Wouldn't it be nice if,
> Coming home was everyone's most important part of every day?

Wouldn't it be nice if,

Every grandmother was thrilled at the sound of her grandchild asking "can I come over"?

Wouldn't it be nice if,

Parents love and grandparents love was the same caring love?

Wouldn't it be nice if,

Parents wanted good grades for their children for the sake of the children and not to impress the community?

Wouldn't it be nice if,

Grandparents could have more than just a few rights?

Wouldn't it be nice if,

You could heal the pain that a lot of grandparents have to deal with over their grandchildren?

Wouldn't it be nice if,

Instead of covering for the kids, mothers could have more faith that dad will be understanding?

Wouldn't it be nice if,

A woman could be the kind of parent she expected the father to be?

Wouldn't it be nice if,

A child's safety was the paramount concern of every adult?

Wouldn't it be nice if,
> Kids didn't have to pay for their parent's stupidity?

Wouldn't it be nice if,
> Everyone could be guaranteed clean drinking water and healthy food?

Wouldn't it be nice if,
> By giving a second chance you're not disappointed?

Wouldn't it be nice if,
> Once again you could live devoid of fear?

Wouldn't it be nice if,
> Insurance really insured?

Wouldn't it be nice if,
> Your common sense was worth more than your empty pockets?

Wouldn't it be nice if,
> There was as much joy in making the world a better place, as there is in making money?

Wouldn't it be nice if,
> Some parents were prideful enough to instill in their children a bit more respect for the law?

Wouldn't it be nice if,
> A divorce wasn't the answer?

Wouldn't it be nice if,
> You could skip having children and go directly to having grandchildren?

Wouldn't it be nice if,
> Tomorrow could be three days in a row?

Wouldn't it be nice if,
> Children could be with their parents 7 days a week?

Wouldn't it be nice if,
> A shining light could light more of your way?

Wouldn't it be nice if,
> A trade was equal?

WOULDN'T IT BE NICE IF . . . ?

YOUTH

Wouldn't it be nice if,

> Wisdom could be taught to the youth while young enough to benefit from the shared wisdom?

Wouldn't it be nice if,

> Young people gave the elderly the respect they are going to expect when they are the elders?

Wouldn't it be nice if,

> Children were taught respect defeats disrespect?

Wouldn't it be nice if,

My showing of respect and admiration would not just some of the time, but all of the time gets the same in return?

Wouldn't it be nice if,

Some love by your parents would be guaranteed by you and yours?

Wouldn't it be nice if,

Concern for your fellow man could start at conception?

Wouldn't it be nice if,

The phrase "respect your elders" read respect, listen and learn?

Wouldn't it be nice if,

Teenage girls could bypass the zit stage and move to the next stage?

Wouldn't it be nice if,

Growing up could be passed down with less pain?

Wouldn't it be nice if,

Father's would listen to their children?

Wouldn't it be nice if,

Children could work first, and go to school second?

Wouldn't it be nice if,

A baby's cry could be interpreted into words?

Wouldn't it be nice if,

Parents raised their children instead of letting video games and TV do it?

Wouldn't it be nice if,

Children would be children until adulthood?

Wouldn't it be nice if,

A child's safety was the paramount concern of every adult?

Wouldn't it be nice if,

Having unprotected sex could be reversed?

Wouldn't it be nice if,

Children didn't have to try to raise themselves?

Wouldn't it be nice if,

When I see you again I won't regret it?

Wouldn't it be nice if,

Your loaded gun, was of money?

Wouldn't it be nice if,

A baby's cries could be interpreted into words?

Wouldn't it be nice if,

The children helped by hearts and generous pockets, as adults remember the children of their day?

Wouldn't it be nice if,
> The young could be guaranteed old age?

Wouldn't it be nice if,
> You didn't think you looked as good with your pants sagging as you do with them at waist high?

Wouldn't it be nice if,
> Young at heart is at any age?

Wouldn't it be nice if,
> Young girls as well as young boys did in fact accept the fact that sex is for mature individuals?

Wouldn't it be nice if,
> A telephone call could straighten up your act?

Wouldn't it be nice if,
> You could make a first impression at least 12 times?

Wouldn't it be nice if,
> Death didn't take so many of the young?

Wouldn't it be nice if,
> There wasn't so much energy wasted on the young?

Wouldn't it be nice if,
> Today's kids enjoyed being just that?

Wouldn't it be nice if,
> A child's cry was heard by multiple pairs of ears?

Wouldn't it be nice if,
> An 18 year old had the wisdom of a 50 year old?

Wouldn't it be nice if,
> "Grow up" meant from childhood to adulthood?

WOULDN'T IT BE NICE IF . . . ?

LOVE

Wouldn't it be nice if,
> Everyone had a wife like mine?

Wouldn't it be nice if,
> Everyone could celebrate fifty years of being together?

Wouldn't it be nice if,
> Love and understanding were more understood?

Wouldn't it be nice if,
> The definition of hate I am looking for, is love?

Wouldn't it be nice if,
>
> Hate was only found in the dictionary?

Wouldn't it be nice if,
>
> Everyone understood the basic five words of any conversation: "please", "thank you" and "excuse me"?

Wouldn't it be nice if,
>
> We could view each other inadequacies without harsh thought?

Wouldn't it be nice if,
>
> Your friend was really your friend?

Wouldn't it be nice if,
>
> Every day you told me "I Love You" I just loved you?

Wouldn't it be nice if,
>
> People love likes dogs love—unconditionally?

Wouldn't it be nice if,
>
> Every husband thought his wife to be the example for other wives to follow?

Wouldn't it be nice if,
>
> Each and every time I said "I Love You" it would be received without provisions?

Wouldn't it be nice if,
>
> Your friends forever stayed with you forever?

Wouldn't it be nice if,
> An outreach of love, help and hope was something we each committed to?

Wouldn't it be nice if,
> The self professed lover could luck out and come close to becoming one?

Wouldn't it be nice if,
> You could remodel your marriage and choose what it would look like?

Wouldn't it be nice if,
> The words "I Love You" always included a footnote of "unconditional"?

Wouldn't it be nice if,
> When you said "good morning neighbor" you are addressing the world?

Wouldn't it be nice if,
> When you ask a question, you received the answer with as much respect as that given when the question was asked?

Wouldn't it be nice if,
> Love endured the harassment of time?

Wouldn't it be nice if,
> I could hold you tight from morning till night, and book you passage on an enchanted flight?

Wouldn't it be nice if,

You could daily get a big hug when the pressures of life have pressurized beyond the beyond?

Wouldn't it be nice if,

You watched my back and I watched yours, and we live in a capitalistic democracy of bliss?

Wouldn't it be nice if,

Love beyond parental love was truly unconditional?

Wouldn't it be nice if,

Your problem could be eliminated with a kiss?

Wouldn't it be nice if,

Love could be traded for understanding?

Wouldn't it be nice if,

Your love was considered the greatest gift ever given?

Wouldn't it be nice if,

You could give someone new a chance to be your friend?

Wouldn't it be nice if,

You could be as forgiving as children are?

Wouldn't it be nice if,
> You and yours would have regular sessions to see which could show the most love?

Wouldn't it be nice if,
> When ladies said "yes" it over rules his "no"?

Wouldn't it be nice if,
> Love could grab hate and slap it silly?

Wouldn't it be nice if,
> Friendship was obtained through feelings rather than materialism?

Wouldn't it be nice if,
> A solid breakfast would suppress hatred for most of the day?

Wouldn't it be nice if,
> Knowing you now could be as exciting as when we first met?

Wouldn't it be nice if,
> People didn't do things that needed forgiving?

Wouldn't it be nice if,
> Love was so far ahead that is could never be overtaken by hate?

Wouldn't it be nice if,
> The words "I Love You" really and truly meant "I Love You"?

Wouldn't it be nice if,
> The love for your fellow man was unconditional?

Wouldn't it be nice if,
> The dollars in my wallet equaled the weight of the love in my heart?

Wouldn't it be nice if,
> Death didn't have so much sorrow in its way?

Wouldn't it be nice if,
> I Love You, meant it in the true sense of the words I Love You?

Wouldn't it be nice if,
> Along side of the big red "S" on your chest you had a big red heart?

Wouldn't it be nice if,
> A kind heart never turned selfish?

Wouldn't it be nice if,
> When you and yours said "I Do", you did?

Wouldn't it be nice if,
> You could settle your differences with a big hug?

Wouldn't it be nice if,
> A heartbeat away was a short distance?

Wouldn't it be nice if,
> All marriages were forever?

Wouldn't it be nice if,
> The key to your heart was in my pocket?

Wouldn't it be nice if,
> The ring on your finger was at least the size
> as the ring in your nose?

Wouldn't it be nice if,
> The love for your fellow man was
> unconditional?

Wouldn't it be nice if,
> Your need to need would be fulfilled by
> someone you need?

Wouldn't it be nice if,
> When you meet the right one it won't
> just be love at first sight, it will be love
> forever?

Wouldn't it be nice if,
> Love didn't come in so many forms: good,
> bad, ugly etc?

Wouldn't it be nice if,
> You men didn't look at your mate as just
> another woman?

WOULDN'T IT BE NICE IF . . . ?

HUMOR

Wouldn't it be nice if,
> When you put your foot in your mouth it could be removed just as easy?

Wouldn't it be nice if,
> A 15 minute power nap did more than just pissed you off?

Wouldn't it be nice if,
> Deodorant could take the place of hot water?

Wouldn't it be nice if,
> Your toe didn't hurt when someone dropped fifty lbs or more on it?

Wouldn't it be nice if,
> Your boyfriend didn't have a girlfriend?

Wouldn't it be nice if,
> A hot shower could wash away your sins?

Wouldn't it be nice if,
> A smoke detector could detect smokers and
> force them to stop smoking?

Wouldn't it be nice if,
> A runny nose actually ran away?

Wouldn't it be nice if,
> You could drive around in park, and on a
> flat tire?

Wouldn't it be nice if,
> When a mosquito bit you, you could bite
> it back?

Wouldn't it be nice if,
> A slap on the back and the expression "buddy
> have a drink" meant buddy have a drink?

Wouldn't it be nice if,
> A pair of pants, were actually two?

Wouldn't it be nice if,
> To see a light at the end of the tunnel really
> meant more than an oncoming train?

Wouldn't it be nice if,
> Your car could run on thoughts?

Wouldn't it be nice if,
>Short cake was a little longer?

Wouldn't it be nice if,
>The expression "it isn't over until a fat lady sings" meant the fat lady really could sing?

Wouldn't it be nice if,
>You could in fact walk in another individual's shoes and therefore have some insight in to what he or she is all about?

Wouldn't it be nice if,
>Daylight savings time, actually saved time?

Wouldn't it be nice if,
>The yellow was green and the blue was orange?

Wouldn't it be nice if,
>Yellow snow wasn't colored by animals?

Wouldn't it be nice if,
>You would leave, people alone, keep your hands to yourself and go back home?

Wouldn't it be nice if,
>When the man at the bank said goodbye and shook your hand, your approved loan contract was in it?

Wouldn't it be nice if,
>We drove off the top ½ of our gas tank instead of the bottom ½?

Wouldn't it be nice if,
>CD's could really see D's?

Wouldn't it be nice if,
>We could look at each other admittedly and say "your best interest is in fact mine"?

Wouldn't it be nice if,
>When the statement "I said no" was used, the involvement in motion, was over?

Wouldn't it be nice if,
>Everyone could turn to someone and say "you are one of the finest people I've met"?

Wouldn't it be nice if,
>When someone showed you the finger it would be to give you directions?

Wouldn't it be nice if,
>An eyesore was nothing more than a sore eye?

Wouldn't it be nice if,
>Each and everyone born today would in fact make it to adulthood unmolested, un-arrested and without receiving a societal beat down?

Wouldn't it be nice if,
>Running shoes helped you run away from your problems?

Wouldn't it be nice if,
> Getting it together really meant you would get it together?

Wouldn't it be nice if,
> One could lose weight as fast as you put it on?

Wouldn't it be nice if,
> Scratching didn't make you itch again?

Wouldn't it be nice if,
> A car like yours could be purchased for less than a king's ransom?

Wouldn't it be nice if,
> Some people would rather be paid cash to tell the truth rather than lie on credit?

Wouldn't it be nice if,
> A driver's license meant you could?

Wouldn't it be nice if,
> You could sing well enough to?

Wouldn't it be nice if,
> What you have on your mind was worth cash?

Wouldn't it be nice if,
> You could open the windows and get a fresh breath of air?

Wouldn't it be nice if,
> When your legs are tired you could remove them and take a break?

Wouldn't it be nice if,
> When I closed my eyes and clicked my heels, it wouldn't hurt so much?

Wouldn't it be nice if,
> Adding more water to the soup pot could also stretch ones intelligence?

Wouldn't it be nice if,
> A dogs bark could alert you as to how stupid you were about to act?

Wouldn't it be nice if,
> Up was down and down was up, so you could never fall down?

Wouldn't it be nice if,
> You could shave today and be hairless next week?

Wouldn't it be nice if,
> The hair that grew down on your face would grow up on the bald spot on your head?

Wouldn't it be nice if,
> Knowing tomorrow was as well known as yesterday?

Wouldn't it be nice if,
> The expression "none of the above" covered the below and around?

Wouldn't it be nice if,
> The yes could remain yes long enough to be accepted?

Wouldn't it be nice if,
> You could get a hundred dollars worth of nickels for fifty dollars?

Wouldn't it be nice if,
> You reached in your pant pocket and found a hundred dollar bill, and they were really your pants?

Wouldn't it be nice if,
> When you ask a stranger to "please pray for me", you wouldn't look like a nut?

Wouldn't it be nice if,
> Ten dollars was for real worth ten dollars?

Wouldn't it be nice if,
> The statement "may I have your attention please", would?

Wouldn't it be nice if,
> Your locked door could give you locked in peace of mind?

Wouldn't it be nice if,
> "Please", "may I" and "thank you" were the three musketeers everyone once new so well?

Wouldn't it be nice if,
> The money in your pocket was really yours?

Wouldn't it be nice if,
> A foot long hot dog could be stretched to 14 inches?

Wouldn't it be nice if,
> People trying to drive on ice, could?

Wouldn't it be nice if,
> A tap on the noggin would do more than just remind you, "You could have had a V8"?

Wouldn't it be nice if,
> Long hair was long lasting?

Wouldn't it be nice if,
> A trampoline could bounce some sense into your head?

Wouldn't it be nice if,
> You could be compensated for not doing dumb things?

Wouldn't it be nice if,
> A footprint could also write?

Wouldn't it be nice if,
> Washing your mouth with soap would also clean up your words?

Wouldn't it be nice if,
> A pair of pants were actually two?

Wouldn't it be nice if,
> Stupidity wasn't such a virtue?

Wouldn't it be nice if,
> An apple a day didn't cost so much?

Wouldn't it be nice if,
> Your pay envelope contained just a little more?

Wouldn't it be nice if,
> Your boss really, really appreciated your talents?

Wouldn't it be nice if,
> Your thin steak was a little thicker?

Wouldn't it be nice if,
> The hole in your shoe would have delayed its growth for just a while longer?

Wouldn't it be nice if,
> That dog bite you received was just in your imagination?

Wouldn't it be nice if,
> Sometime your imagination wasn't yours?

Wouldn't it be nice if,
> Two one dollar bills side by side added up to eleven dollars?

Wouldn't it be nice if,
> Removing a growth from your throat is a tonsillectomy, a removing of a growth from your side is an appendectomy and removing a growth from your head was only a haircut?

Wouldn't it be nice if,
> When your rubbed elbows it didn't peel the skin off?

Wouldn't it be nice if,
> A knuckle sandwich was nutritious?

Wouldn't it be nice if,
> When you scratched your head the dandruff didn't remind you so much of winter?

Wouldn't it be nice if,
> Your legs were as big as your eyes?

Wouldn't it be nice if,
> A grumpy neighbor wasn't?

Wouldn't it be nice if,
> Gas was less than a house payment?

Wouldn't it be nice if,
> A broken toe could be repaired with super glue?

Wouldn't it be nice if,
> A scratch today wouldn't be an itch tomorrow?

Wouldn't it be nice if,
> "Good morning" meant that's what it was going to be?

Wouldn't it be nice if,
> A rubber band could stretch the imagination?

Wouldn't it be nice if,
> You finally put your shoes on the right feet and it turns out those are the shoes you meant to wear?

WOULDN'T IT BE NICE IF . . . ?

POLITICS

Wouldn't it be nice if,
> Freedom was truly free?

Wouldn't it be nice if,
> Our government was truly ours?

Wouldn't it be nice if,
> A politicians worth could in fact be measured by his or her words?

Wouldn't it be nice if,
> The President has as much respect for the people as the people have for the President?

Wouldn't it be nice if,
>
> We created a 51st state and it was void of problems?

Wouldn't it be nice if,
>
> The governors of whatever State would put as much effort in running his or her state as he or she does in attracting negative press?

Wouldn't it be nice if,
>
> "We the People" truly was from the people?

Wouldn't it be nice if,
>
> You didn't have to worry about terrorist?

Wouldn't it be nice if,
>
> Every country could be as disciplined as the United States?

Wouldn't it be nice if,
>
> People would talk about the future, three to four times as much as they talk about the past?

Wouldn't it be nice if,
>
> A dollar bill and a five dollar bill added up to fifteen dollars?

Wouldn't it be nice if,
>
> The United States was large enough to hold all of the alien traffic?

Wouldn't it be nice if,
>
> The word "government", meant ticket to a life of milk and honey?

Wouldn't it be nice if,
> Health care meant it?

Wouldn't it be nice if,
> Your back could have the same protection as your front?

Wouldn't it be nice if,
> When the President spoke, the country listens?

Wouldn't it be nice if,
> Politicians could be less political?

Wouldn't it be nice if,
> Republicans weren't so greedy?

Wouldn't it be nice if,
> People would admit there are things just as important or more so, than money?

Wouldn't it be nice if,
> Giving more freedom made you less stupid?

Wouldn't it be nice if,
> The president was for all the people?

Wouldn't it be nice if,
> Sarah Palin was *Sarah Go Away?*

Wouldn't it be nice if,
> Alaskans had never heard of Sarah Palin?

Wouldn't it be nice if,

> The respect for the United States and its neighbors, could last forever?

Wouldn't it be nice if,

> Grass was just as green (or greener) than it is on the other side?

Wouldn't it be nice if,

> Politics could be spelled with a heart—poli (heart) tics?

Wouldn't it be nice if,

> Gas prices dropped until employment improved?

WOULDN'T IT BE NICE IF . . . ?

INSPIRATIONAL

Wouldn't it be nice if,
> People loved people more than they loved themselves?

Wouldn't it be nice if,
> Everyone was treated like someone because someone is related to someone else?

Wouldn't it be nice if,
> People understood, people can change the world—and it begins with me?

Wouldn't it be nice if,
> People understood the positive impact of a smile and a kind word, and it costs you nothing?

Wouldn't it be nice if,
> Mankind could be friends forever, unconditionally?

Wouldn't it be nice if,
> Everyone looked at others the way they wanted to be looked at?

Wouldn't it be nice if,
> The sun shined down on you and you shined your rays of sunlight on those needing a brighter day?

Wouldn't it be nice if,
> The cares of the world, were those of the people of the world?

Wouldn't it be nice if,
> Civil rights were adopted by all? (People would be more civil.)

Wouldn't it be nice if,
> God was in everyone's heart?

Wouldn't it be nice if,
> The concerns shared by you and yours, actually made a difference?

Wouldn't it be nice if,
> When God talks to you, you listen?

Wouldn't it be nice if,
> Healing the world was something we all participated in?

Wouldn't it be nice if,
> Doing more with less included being better?

Wouldn't it be nice if,
> Your neighbor really and truly enjoyed being your neighbor?

Wouldn't it be nice if,
> People didn't do the thing that needed forgiving?

Wouldn't it be nice if,
> All religions agreed on the basic truths?

Wouldn't it be nice if,
> A child new the meaning of "Thank You Jesus" before they could say it?

Wouldn't it be nice if,
> We as a people judged more of ourselves and less of others?

Wouldn't it be nice if,
> Everyone could admit God is in fact love?

Wouldn't it be nice if,
> My "brother's keeper" weren't just words?

Wouldn't it be nice if,
> People were colorblind with regards to ethnicity?

Wouldn't it be nice if,

>Gender barriers were removed from the world?

Wouldn't it be nice if,

>Respect wasn't found exclusively in the dictionary?

Wouldn't it be nice if,

>All hearts were pumping the same level of caring?

Wouldn't it be nice if,

>A calculator could figure out how many positive days you would have each week?

Wouldn't it be nice if,

>There was a dictionary with only definitions of happiness?

Wouldn't it be nice if,

>When you greeted someone with a handshake you felt warm all over?

Wouldn't it be nice if,

>Everyone who has received help from someone, passed that help on to someone else?

Wouldn't it be nice if,

>Every morning you awake, you give thanks to awaking to another morning of God's life?

Wouldn't it be nice if,
> Kindness and courtesy were as popular as sports?

Wouldn't it be nice if,
> There were eyeglasses that would only let you see the good in people?

Wouldn't it be nice if,
> Oprah's passion for helping humanity was contagious to the point of engaging 100 percent human involvement?

Wouldn't it be nice if,
> Someday one of the definitions for "human kindness" was Oprah?

Wouldn't it be nice if,
> Give me a leg up automatically meant success?

Wouldn't it be nice if,
> GOD were in everyone's heart?

Wouldn't it be nice if,
> The other cheek didn't hurt so badly?

Wouldn't it be nice if,
> You would love all children with the same enthusiasm as you love your own?

Wouldn't it be nice if,
> Putting a floor under your knee meant God was listening?

Wouldn't it be nice if,
> The statement was "GOD bless the world", and not just America?

Wouldn't it be nice if,
> Everyone could admit that GOD is in fact love?

Wouldn't it be nice if,
> If the words "I am my brother's keeper "weren't just words?

Wouldn't it be nice if,
> Everyone was absent of heartache?

Wouldn't it be nice if,
> A battery could energize your soul?

Wouldn't it be nice if,
> Prayer was guaranteed to change one for the better?

Wouldn't it be nice if,
> A fallen star could crush all negativity?

Wouldn't it be nice if,
> "Help, hope and inspiration" swept our nation with the same intensity as a national disaster?

Wouldn't it be nice if,
> You could be the fastest problem solver in the west?

Wouldn't it be nice if,
>   Being a human being meant you had a good heart?

Wouldn't it be nice if,
>   The gifts God has given us were put to work to make a positive difference in our world?

Wouldn't it be nice if,
>   The devil had more enemies and fewer friends?

Wouldn't it be nice if,
>   My Lord Jesus was everyone's?

Wouldn't it be nice if,
>   Everyone was nice?

Wouldn't it be nice if,
>   A perfect world was something you looked forward to?

Wouldn't it be nice if,
>   A camera could take pictures of your soul?

Wouldn't it be nice if,
>   Global thinking began at home?

Wouldn't it be nice if,
>   Selflessness was the beginning of kindness, helpfulness, caring, understanding, etc.?

Wouldn't it be nice if,
>Wisdom could be had in other ways other than living life?

Wouldn't it be nice if,
>I could leave you here and at the same time take you with me (to heaven)?

Wouldn't it be nice if,
>The trust you have in me could be reinforced by the trust I have in you?

Wouldn't it be nice if,
>Nice could be packaged and sold?

Wouldn't it be nice if,
>I could wave my hand over your head and fill it with nothing but positives?

Wouldn't it be nice if,
>Oprah could be cloned?

Wouldn't it be nice if,
>People could remember to look at life from other people's perspective—at least some times?

Wouldn't it be nice if,
>There were more smiles in the world, than there are frowns?

Wouldn't it be nice if,
>Speaking your mind meant friendship across the world?

Wouldn't it be nice if,
> The calm before the storm continued through the storm?

Wouldn't it be nice if,
> There were more random acts of kindness than there are random acts of violence?

Wouldn't it be nice if,
> Everyone affected the price of freedom?

Wouldn't it be nice if,
> The hands of time would run a little slow?

Wouldn't it be nice if,
> When you said "hello" you mean your contribution to humanity is greatly appreciated?

Wouldn't it be nice if,
> All there were to life was living it?

Wouldn't it be nice if,
> Nice lived in our hearts—365 days a year—wouldn't it be nice?

BIOGRAPHY

BILLY RAY MACON SR.

Born January 28, 1942 in Marshall Texas to Tommie and Arneda Macon, the family moved to Oakland, CA. At 14, he worked in Alaska (while still a territory) until returning to Oakland in 1956. On June 12, 1959 he wed Lourdes Campos, immediately relocated to Anchorage where they reside today. Father of 4, Grandfather of 11 and Great Grandfather of 2; his hobbies include family time, writing, drawing, travel, laughing!

Billy believes the art of writing is a very powerful and personal way to touch others. "..... I am grateful for this opportunity to connect with readers around the Globe."

.

Made in the USA
Lexington, KY
14 December 2010